Sketches of Durham C

Margot Smith

Ivan Corbett · Truro

The Viaduct.

The Market Place.

View from the Station

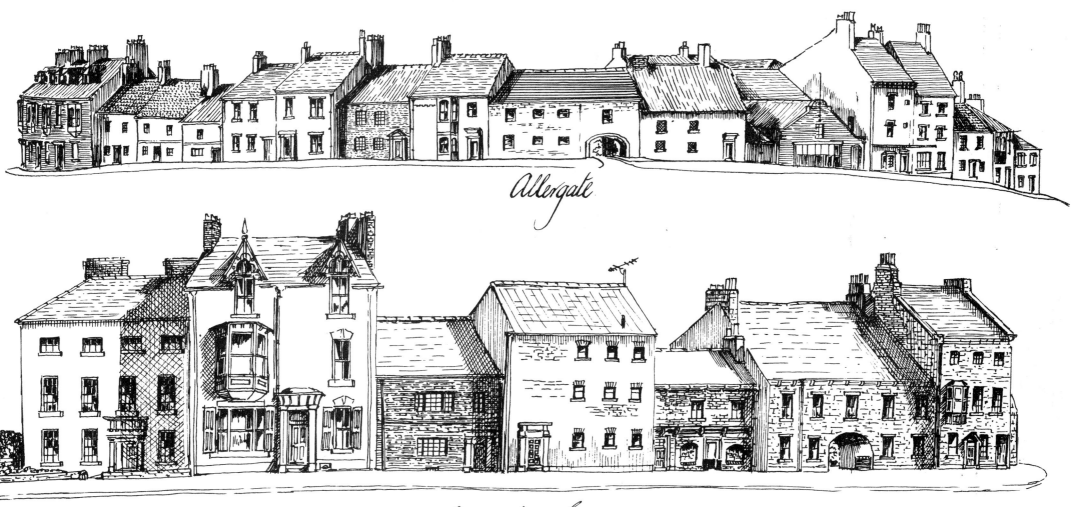

Allergate

Church Street.

The Black Staircase, Kentiam Castle.

The Tithe Barn

St. Nicholas' Church.

The Durham Teapot

Saddler Street.

Old houses, Elvet Bridge.

The Cathedral

South Street.

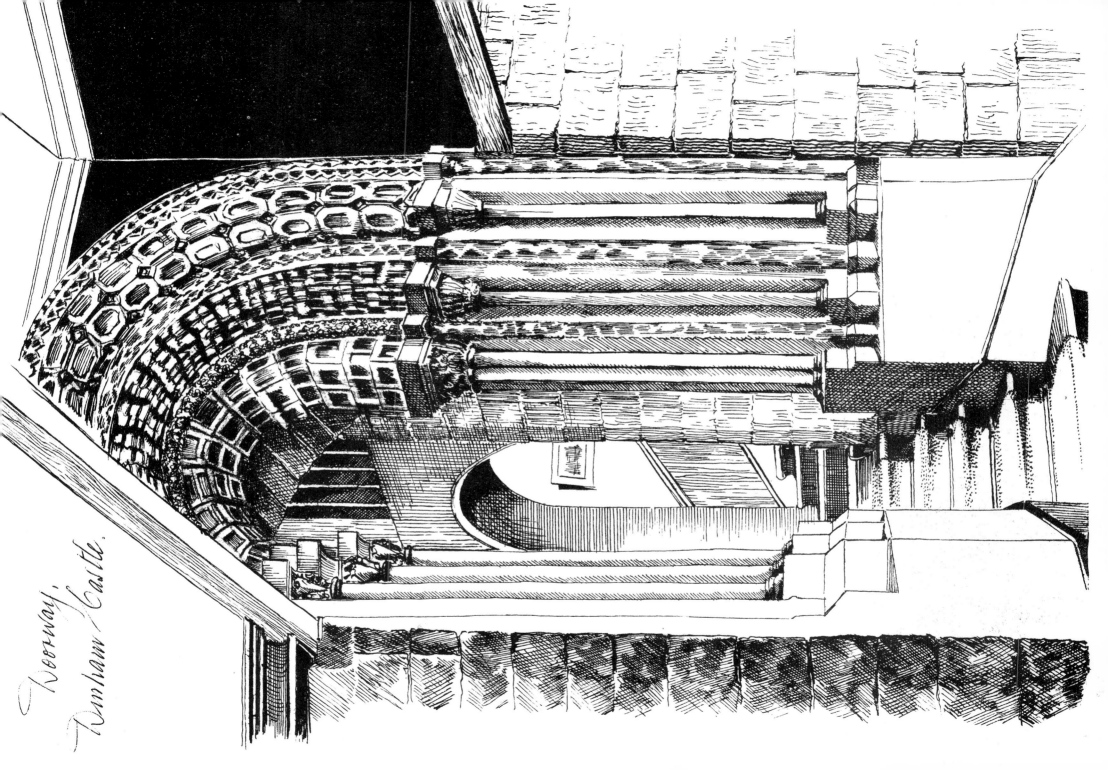

Doorway,
Durham Castle.

St. Godric's Church.

CROOK HALL

MARGOT
SMITH
1975.

The Watergate

St Mary-the-Less

Prebends' Bridge

St. Oswald's Church.

Durham Willow Pattern.

Old Elvet

The Gatehouse of The Kepier Hospital, built in 1341 - all that remains of an institution founded by Bishop Flambard in the 12th Century.

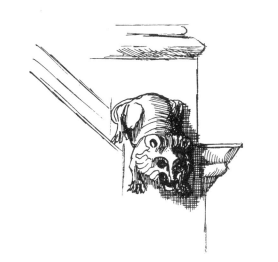

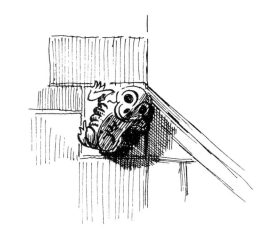

Claypath and some carvings from St Nicholas' Church.

Dunelm House

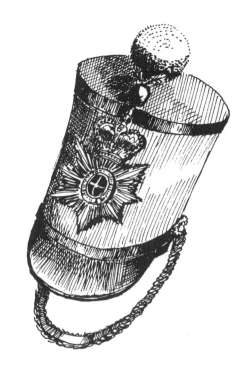

The Regimental Crest of the
Durham Light Infantry
(disbanded in 1968),
and headgear associated
with the Regiment
from the early 19th Century.
(The D.L.I. Museum).

View of St Margarets

Leazes Place

Houses in the North Bailey

View from Pelaw Woods

ISBN 0 904836 12 6
© 1981 Margot Smith

First published 1975
New Edition 1981 by Ivan Corbett
Cove Hill, Perran-ar-Worthal, Truro, Cornwall.

Printing by City Printing Works (Chester-le-Street) Ltd.,
Broadwood View, Chester-le-Street, Co. Durham.

Left: Doorway, St. Cuthbert's Society, South Bailey

Front Cover: St. Cuthbert's Pectoral Cross, Treasury Museum

Back Cover: Sanctuary Knocker - Cathedral

Title Page: Dun Cow — Cathedral

Acknowledgements: The Church of England; Master of University College; Dr. and Mrs. Hawgood of Crook Hall; Dean and Chapter, Durham Cathedral.